FREIGHTERS

FREIG

Thomas Y. Crowell   New York

HELLENIC LINES

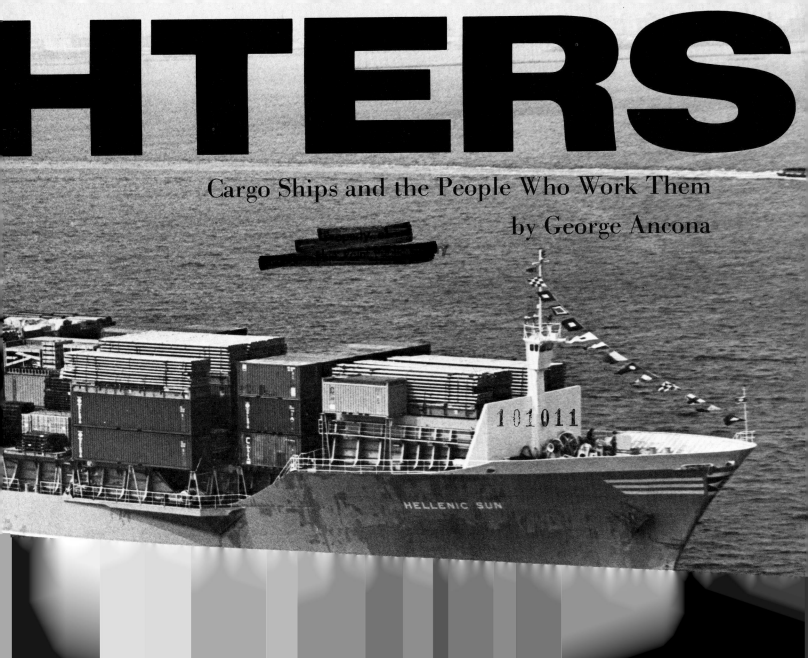

HTERS

Cargo Ships and the People Who Work Them

by George Ancona

HELLENIC SUN

101011

To little Helge

Freighters: Cargo Ships and the People Who Work Them
Copyright © 1985 by George Ancona
All rights reserved. Printed in the U.S.A.
1 2 3 4 5 6 7 8 9 10
First Edition

Library of Congress Cataloging in Publication Data
Ancona, George.
    Freighters : cargo ships and the people who work
them.

    Summary: A photo essay describing the various
types of cargo ships, how they operate, and the jobs
of the crews that maintain them.

    1. Cargo ships—Juvenile literature. 2. Merchant
seamen—Juvenile literature. [1. Cargo ships.
2. Ships. 3. Merchant seamen. 4. Occupations]
1. Title.
VM391.A48 1985   623.8′245   83-45059
ISBN 0-690-04358-9
ISBN 0-690-04359-7 (lib. bdg.)

A giant freighter cuts through the harbor waters. It dwarfs the tug that guides it against the dock. Lines thrown by the deck crew arc their way to longshoremen, who tie it to the pier. The gangway is lowered, and the stevedores swarm aboard. Cargo loading begins.

INTRODUCTION
Ships need cargoes, and cargoes need ships. The search goes on by teletype in ship brokers' offices:

"...require 150,000-cubic-foot reefer for 1100 tons citrus loading Montevideo 8–11 October for Hamburg..."

"...molybdenum steel from Uddevalla to Baltimore..."

"...raw cotton from Brownsville to Quingdao..."

"...trucks from Constantsa to Valparaiso..."

Freighters of many shapes and sizes will sail these cargoes to distant ports. Some—called liners—sail on regular schedules and routes. Others sail to wherever they can find a cargo. These are the ships called tramps.

The general cargo ship can take a variety of goods packed in a variety of ways. But there are specialized ships for almost everything. The container ship carries a variety of goods that are prepacked in standard-size containers, which speed up the loading and unloading of the ship. Other ships are built to carry

one type of cargo: Liquids are carried in tankers, perishables in reefers and vehicles in drive-aboard ro-ros.

The men and women who go to sea have more safety and comfort than their ancestors did on old-time sailing ships. But some things are still the same. There is still the routine of life at sea. Once a crew signs on a ship, they will be on board for months, performing the same jobs every day. And there are still dangers and emergencies to be alert for. Shipmates must rely on each other: If anything goes wrong at sea, no one else can be called in to fix it.

CONTENTS

THE SHIP The shell, or hull, of a ship is designed to cut through water and provide stability in rolling seas. Modern steel hulls are constructed to bend and twist under the stresses of cargoes, heat and ocean swells...otherwise they would snap in two.

Deep in the hull is the engine room, which houses either a steam or a diesel engine. A revolving shaft runs from the engine out through the stern end of the ship. The shaft transfers power from the engine to the propeller (the screw). The turning of the propeller moves the ship through the water. Some ships have two propellers, or twin screws, which make the ship more maneuverable. Behind the propeller is the rudder, the flat vertical panel that steers the ship.

The rest of the hull is sectioned vertically by bulkheads into holds where the cargo is stored. The hull is divided horizontally by decks. The deeper the hull, the more decks it will have. When there is only one deck below the top deck, the space between is

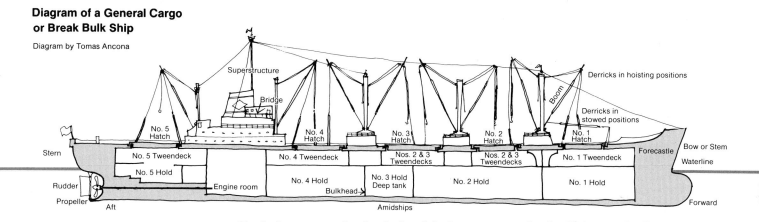

Diagram of a General Cargo or Break Bulk Ship

Diagram by Tomas Ancona

Superstructure

Bridge

Derricks in hoisting positions

Boom

Derricks in stowed positions

No. 5 Hatch

No. 4 Hatch

No. 3 Hatch

No. 2 Hatch

No. 1 Hatch

Forecastle

Bow or Stem

Stern

Waterline

No. 5 Tweendeck

No. 4 Tweendeck

Nos. 2 & 3 Tweendecks

Nos. 2 & 3 Tweendecks

No. 1 Tweendeck

Rudder

No. 5 Hold

Engine room

No. 4 Hold

No. 3 Hold Deep tank

No. 2 Hold

No. 1 Hold

Propeller

Bulkhead

Aft

Amidships

Forward

called the tweendeck. A double bottom in the hull forms ballast tanks: When the ship is sailing without a cargo, seawater is pumped into them to give the ship more weight and stability.

Derricks mounted on the top deck raise and lower cargo into the holds through the hatchways. Watertight hatch covers keep the cargo dry.

Rising above the top deck is the superstructure. On its top level is the navigating bridge, from which the ship is controlled. Below are the officers' and crew's quarters, passenger cabins, galley (kitchen), ship's stores (supplies) and machine shops.

A net lashed from the ship to the dock catches any sacks that may fall off the sling. The sacks of coffee are placed on a wood platform called a pallet. A forklift moves the pallet into the warehouse. This is an expensive method of unloading—it takes a lot of time and hard work, and there's a high risk of damage or theft.

CONTAINER SHIP

Containers have revolutionized the world of shipping. Instead of loading a jumble of individual crates, bales and barrels, this ship carries only containers. A container is a standard-size (8′ x 8′ x 20′ or 8′ x 8′ x 40′) steel box in which a variety of goods are shipped. The container is prepacked at a farm or factory, sealed and taken by truck or train to the seaport. It remains sealed until it arrives at its destination overseas. This reduces breakage or theft of the contents. Instead of a large gang of stevedores, a small crew with one person operating a giant gantry crane can do the loading.

Containerization has changed the shapes of ships and seaports. Ports need larger open storage areas for stacking containers. Longer docks with movable gantry cranes have been built to accommodate the longer ships—the ships are built longer rather than wider because they have to be able to go through the Panama Canal. (Sometimes a conventional ship is simply cut in

Hellenic Sun

DWT	23,417 tons
LOA	627′ (191.16m)
Beam	78′9″ (24m)
Speed	17 knots
Engine	Diesel
Capacity	1200 20′ containers (or 600 40′ containers)

15

American Trader

DWT	29,749 tons
LOA	820' (249.94m)
Beam	100'2" (30.53m)
Speed	22 knots
Engine	Steam
Capacity	1858 20' containers
	(or 929 40' containers)

half and a midsection added.) To make more room on deck for containers, the superstructures are positioned forward or aft.

Once the container ship is in port, two giant shoreside gantry cranes on rails move alongside. One crane unloads, while the other loads new cargo, getting the job done in hours instead of days. The crane operator up in the gantry lowers a heavy steel frame with fittings that lock onto the container. The container is lifted off the trailer chassis and lowered into cells in the ship's hold. These cells keep the stacked containers from sliding around.

When the hold is filled, the hatches are covered, and more containers are stacked and lashed to the deck. To keep the ship level and prevent heeling over while loading, water is pumped in or out of the ballast tanks to compensate for the shifting weight.

Containerization has greatly reduced the time a ship must stay in port. It can now spend more time at sea, which is what a ship is designed to do.

RO-RO

Newly manufactured cars and trucks are shipped to ports around the world in freighters called ro-ros. Until the invention of the ro-ro, cranes had to be used to hoist the vehicles on board. It was a slow process and a risky one too—sometimes cars were dropped or damaged in other ways. To speed up the loading, ships are now designed to allow cars and trucks to roll on and roll off under their own power. Hence the name "ro-ro."

This ro-ro, the *Hual Trader*, has eleven decks. Six of them can be adjusted to accommodate vehicles of different heights. The cars are loaded by means of two angled stern ramps, one on each side of the ship.

Hual Trader

DWT	32,772 tons
LOA	697' (212.44m)
Beam	105'11" (32.293m)
Speed	17 knots
Engine	Diesel
Capacity	5992 small cars
	159 trailers
	1203 containers

For the unloading operation, a bus takes a team of drivers onto the ship. In a few minutes a line of cars comes zooming down the ramp. The bus then follows to pick up the drivers in the parking area. This is repeated until the ship is completely unloaded.

Now the ship is ready to take on new cargo. Farm machinery, container trucks and other wheeled equipment will be driven up the ramps, and the ship will begin its return journey.

CONTAINER RO-RO

Atlantic Saga

DWT	14,872 tons
LOA	731' (222.80m)
Beam	98' (29.87m)
Speed	19 knots
Engine	Diesel
Capacity	862 20' containers
	890 compact cars
	and 164 20' trucks

The container ro-ro is specially designed to make maximum use of all space on board. Two types of cargo can be carried in this one multipurpose ship. While cars and rolling stock are being driven up the stern ramps, gantry cranes can be loading containers onto the forward end.

Since a ship's hull is curved and containers are rectangular, there is extra space around the containers that on an ordinary container ship would go to waste. In the container ro-ro, this space is used to store automobiles, helicopters—any odd-shaped

ATLANTIC SAGA
GÖTEBORG

cargo on wheels. An entire circus with cages, vans and trailers has been transported to and from Europe in this manner.

As on the ro-ro, the decks can be adjusted for different heights. The top deck, too, can be used for stacking containers.

Snow Storm

DWT	15,719 tons
LOA	524'11" (159.72m)
Beam	80'11" (24.66m)
Speed	22 knots
Engine	Diesel
Capacity	611,615 cubic feet
	(17,125 cubic meters)

REEFER Fruits and vegetables, meats and fish—all of these perishable goods can be shipped around the world in the refrigerated holds of the reefer ship. Temperatures in these holds can be lowered to freezing. The holds are heavily insulated, and often the ships are painted white to reflect the sun's heat.

Down in the holds, sensors monitor the temperature. The information is transmitted to computers in the engine room and on the bridge, where it is checked by the officers on each watch.

Here in the hold of the *Snow Storm*, boxes of bananas are placed on a conveyor that will carry them to the dock. This ship can also use its own derricks to lift cargo.

American Republic
(Great Lakes ship)

DWT	54,000 tons
LOA	634'10" (193.27m)
Beam	68' (20.72m)
Speed	13 knots
Engine	Diesel
Capacity	20,000 tons
Unloading rate	6000 tons per hour

BULK CARRIER   Coal, phosphates, ores, fertilizers and grains are called bulk products. These cargoes are free-flowing—they can be poured directly into the holds of ships. Ships that carry coal in this way are called colliers.

Crossing the Great Lakes of North America are the uniquely designed bulk carriers that bring iron ore and coal from the west to the industrial east: the Great Lakes ships.

The larger of the Great Lakes ships measure up to 1000′ (304.80m), the length of 3⅓ football fields. They are built narrower than ocean-going bulk carriers because they must pass through the narrow channels between lakes.

The newer Great Lakes ships are capable of unloading their own cargo. Hoppers at the bottom of each hold drop the ore onto conveyor belts that run the length of the ship. The belts carry the ore up to a boom that extends over the stockpile on the dock. The ore is transferred to the boom's conveyor, which drops it into the stockpile.

Ocean-going bulk carriers are built more sturdily to withstand heavy ocean swells. These swells would break up a Great Lakes ore carrier. Here an Indian ship is loaded with scrap iron by a giant floating crane.

LASH SHIP

In shallow ports where a large ship cannot get close enough to the docks for loading, goods can be brought out to the ship in prepacked sealed barges called lighters. Tugboats tow these lighters down rivers and out into harbors. There, out in the deep water, a LASH ship waits. This ship doesn't need a dock. The built-in gantry crane in its stern lifts the lighters on board. The name LASH stands for *L*ighter *A*board *SH*ip.

Almost anything can be loaded into these watertight lighters. Like containers, they can carry machinery, refrigerated perishables or bulk cargo.

LASH Atlantico

DWT	39,564 tons
LOA	820' (249.29m)
Beam	100' (30.48m)
Speed	20 knots
Engine	Steam
Capacity	32 lighters
	and 822 20' containers

Every fifteen minutes a tug pushes a lighter under the gantry crane. The lighters are lifted out of the water, moved down the length of the ship and stacked and locked one on top of the other.

Where ports are deeper, the LASH ship can come right up to the docks. A crane in the forward part of the ship loads containers on deck or into the hold.

TANKER Bulk carriers that transport liquids are called tankers. These ships carry petroleum products, chemicals and various foods such as frozen citrus juice. Ships that carry a variety of products are called "drugstores."

The hull of the tanker is divided into a series of tanks along its length and beam. The separate tanks keep the cargo from sloshing about dangerously and tipping the ship at sea.

Crude oil tankers—ships that carry raw petroleum to the refineries—are the giants of the seas. As oil exporting has grown, bigger tankers have been built. A huge tanker can carry more product than a smaller tanker, without an increase in crew. Today we have Very Large Crude Carriers (VLCC) of 250,000 DWT and Ultra Large Crude Carriers (ULCC), the largest being 542,000 DWT.

There are very few ports deep enough to accommodate these supertankers. Cargo must be transferred to smaller tankers, or loaded and unloaded through submerged pipes that run out from shore.

Once crude oil has been refined into various petroleum products (gasoline, heating oil, jet fuel, etc.), these are piped to special tankers that will distribute them. Like floating gas stations, these tankers sail up the coast delivering cargo.

The tanker *Rhode Island* has nine holds, each divided into three tanks: port, center and starboard. It carries several petroleum products. Here the shore crew together with the deck crew hook up the giant hoses that lead to the tanks on shore. Pumps aboard the ship will discharge the cargo.

Before the ship returns to the refinery, its tanks will be cleaned. The waste water and oils will be saved and reprocessed to prevent pollution. The tanks are filled with seawater to serve as ballast.

Gerona (On previous page)

DWT	170,528 tons
LOA	950′ (285.29m)
Beam	150′ (46.2m)
Speed	15 knots
Engine	Steam
Capacity	1,135,000 barrels

Rhode Island

DWT	26,550 tons
LOA	604′8″ (184.31m)
Beam	78′4″ (23.88m)
Speed	17½ knots
Engine	Steam
Capacity	208,134 barrels

LNG TANKER

An increased demand for natural gas has brought about the design of a new ship, the LNG tanker. LNG stands for Liquefied Natural Gas: Before it is shipped, the gas is cooled down to −260° Fahrenheit or −129° Centigrade. This reduces it to a liquid state, which is easier to transport. One cubic foot of liquefied gas is equal to 620 cubic feet of natural gas. Now only one tanker is needed to carry 125,000 cubic feet of LNG—enough to heat 19,000 homes for a year. At its destination, the liquid is heated and reconverted to gas.

The LNG is carried in five aluminum spheres. These tanks are insulated to keep the LNG cold. As some of the liquid warms during the trip, it turns back into gas, which can be used by the ship's power plant as additional fuel.

Lake Charles

DWT	93,500 tons
LOA	936' (285.29m)
Beam	143' (43.58m)
Speed	20 knots
Engine	Steam
Capacity	4,412,500 cubic feet
	(125,000 cubic meters)
	(equal to 157,200 barrels)

THE SHIP'S CREW

This is the crew of the tanker *Rhode Island*, one of a fleet of ships that sail the coasts from Maine to Alaska and Hawaii. Most of the crew have been sailing together for several years. The *officers (above)* are on board for two months, and off for two months. The rest of the crew sign on for each voyage.

The ship operates twenty-four hours a day, seven days a week, at sea or in port. The crew's work is divided into watches of four hours, each followed by eight hours off. The six watches are from twelve to four, four to eight and eight to twelve, A.M. and P.M.

The crew is made up of three departments.

The *deck department* consists of the officers—the captain, the first, second and third mates, the radio officer and a deck cadet—and the deck crew: the boatswain (pronounced bos'n) and the ablebodied and ordinary seamen.

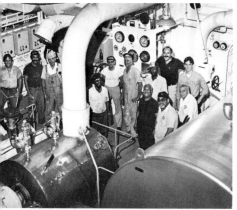

The *engine department* is made up of the chief engineer, the first, second and third assistant engineers, enginemen, wipers, pumpmen and an engineering cadet.

The *stewards' department* consists of the chief steward, the cook, the galley utility men and the cabin steward.

The Deck Department

On the bridge, each mate stands a four-hour watch with an ablebodied seaman at the wheel as "quartermaster," or "helmsman." The course is set by the captain. The mate keeps the ship on course, directing the helmsman by calling out compass points for him to steer by. Every two hours the helmsman is relieved by another seaman. Any problems are reported to the captain, who is always on call.

Officers are either graduates of a merchant marine academy or have "come up the hawsepipe," that is, worked their way up from seaman.

When the ship leaves or arrives at a port, the order "All hands!" is given. Every officer takes a position on deck—first mate on the bow, second astern, third on the bridge with the captain. The rest of the crew are on deck to handle lines, winches and cables for anchoring or tying up.

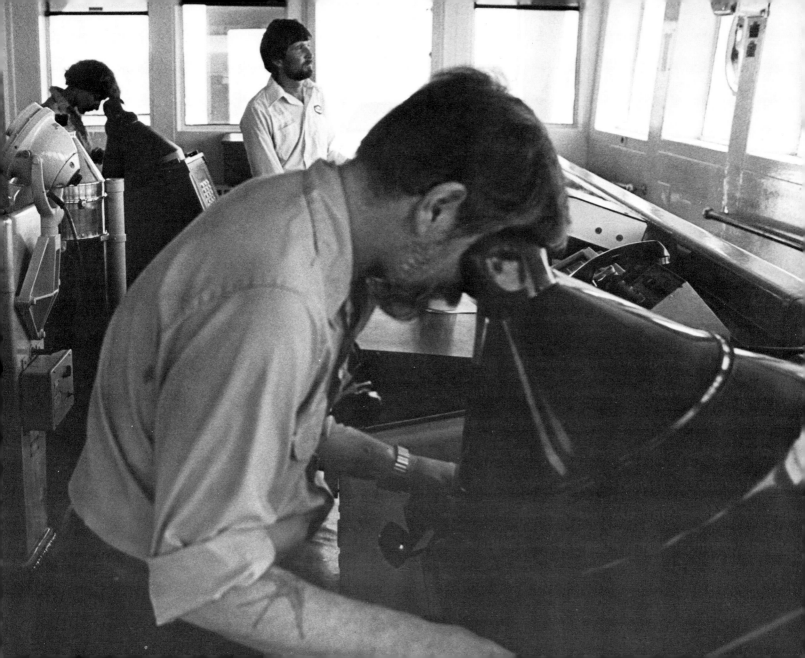

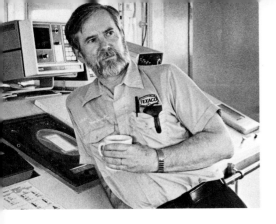

The Deck Officers

The *Captain* is master of the ship and is respectfully referred to as "the old man." He is responsible for the ship's operation and for the safety of the crew and cargo.

The first officer, or *First Mate*, sees that the cargo is loaded properly. He supervises the deck crew and oversees the maintenance of the ship and all equipment. He is also the cadet's instructor.

The *Second Mate* is the navigator. Using compass, loran and radar, and observing the position of the sun, stars and planets, he plots the ship's course. Upkeep and repair of the lifeboats is his job too.

The *Third Mate* directs the discharging of cargo, and maintains lifesaving and firefighting equipment. She also makes out the ship's log, a complete report of all the ship's activities at sea and in port.

The *Radio Officer*, usually called "Sparks," keeps in touch with the ship's owners, with harbors and with other ships. He also listens for SOS signals from ships in distress. He keeps the ship's electronic equipment in good repair.

A *Deck Cadet* is a student of a merchant marine academy who is fulfilling his apprenticeship at sea. On board he does all kinds of deck work. When he graduates from the academy he will have earned a third mate's license along with his degree.

47

The Deck Crew

The *Boatswain (above, left)* is in charge of the deck crew. He reports to the first mate and then assigns the specific jobs to the crew.

Ablebodied Seamen have been trained in seamanship. In addition to doing routine maintenance work they go aloft to work on the rigging. They also perform quartermaster duty.

Ordinary Seamen do the regular maintenance work, such as chipping rust, painting and repairing. On a tanker they also clean the empty tanks and connect the hoses for pumping cargo.

48

The Engine Department

It's the engine crew that keeps the ship moving. They make sure that all the machinery—engines, generators, pumps, compressors, boilers, etc.—is in working order. Among the crew are skilled machinists, engineers, electricians, plumbers, carpenters and welders. They work in the heat, noise and vibration of the engine room.

The *Rhode Island* is powered by a steam engine that burns bunker at the rate of about 440 barrels (18,480 gallons) a day. A huge tank in the hold stores over 550,000 gallons—enough to fuel the ship for more than 25 days. The water that makes the steam in the engine's boiler is distilled from seawater. Generators produce electricity for the entire ship. And should the engine or any of the ship's machinery break down, the machine shop contains all the tools necessary for a repair at sea.

The Engineers

The *Chief Engineer* is the officer in charge of the engine department. He reports directly to the captain. He schedules the watches for the engine crew and orders the fuel, supplies and parts needed to keep the ship moving.

The *First Assistant Engineer* is in charge of the engine room. He sees to it that all work and repairs are done.

The *Second Assistant Engineer* is the boiler expert. He maintains the boiler and keeps the pipes and plumbing in good order.

The *Third Assistant Engineer* specializes in the upkeep of all the lubricating oil systems that keep the machines running smoothly.

An *Engineering Cadet* assists on jobs in the engine room wherever he is needed. His experience on board along with his studies will qualify him for a third engineer's license.

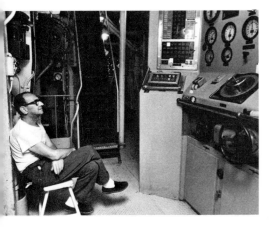

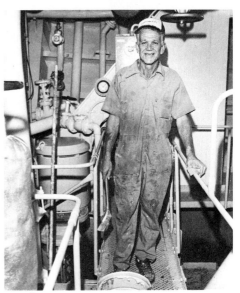

The Engine Crew

The *Enginemen* are the "eyes" of the engineers. They monitor the temperature and pressure gauges that indicate if all the machinery is working properly. Each assistant engineer, together with an engineman, works a four-hour watch in the engine room. It is extremely hot and noisy in the engine room and the crew must shout into each others' ears to be heard.

Wipers lubricate and clean the machinery. They also do the maintenance and painting in the engine room.

Pumpmen operate the pumps that load and discharge the cargo. They care for the network of pipes and tanks on board the tanker.

55

The Stewards' Department

The stewards' department keeps the crew well fed and comfortable. They cook and bake for three meals a day, plus snacks, and prepare the gallons of hot coffee for the breaks. They are also in charge of the housekeeping on board. Keeping a crew of thirty-five supplied with clean linen and maintaining their quarters is like running a hotel.

The *Chief Steward* plans the menus and orders the food and kitchen supplies needed for each voyage. He will buy fresh food whenever the ship is in port. He also works with the cook in the galley.

The *Cook* prepares the three main meals for the crew.

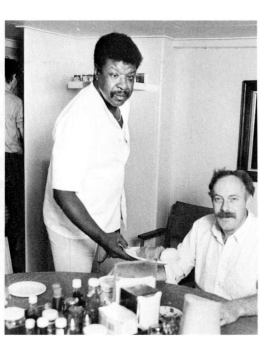

The *Galley Utility Men* help the cooks with the meals and clean up afterward. One serves in the officer's mess (dining room) and the other serves in the crew's mess.

The *Cabin Steward* cleans, makes the beds and straightens up the officers' and passengers' cabins.

OFF DUTY

Life aboard a freighter is rigorous, but there is also time to relax. The off-duty hours are for eating and sleeping, for socializing with shipmates, watching TV or playing games. It's also a time to be alone—to read, write letters, study for exams, fish, exercise...or just watch the sea with its passing ships, spouting whales and soaring birds—and think of the day the voyage ends and it's time to go home.

GLOSSARY

Aft—toward the stern of a ship.

Aloft—up in the rigging of a ship.

Ballast—weight added to a ship to balance it and give it stability in the water. Seawater, pumped into ballast tanks, is most commonly used.

Barge—a flat-bottomed boat with no engine, used to transport cargo. Barges are usually towed or pushed by tugboats.

Bridge—the part of the superstructure where all the navigation controls are.

Bunker—a heavy oil used to fuel ships' engines.

Deck—a floor or platform in a ship. The decks divide the hull into different levels.

Forward—toward the bow of a ship.

Gangway—a staircase or ramp that can be lowered from the side of a ship to the dock. A gangway is used for boarding and leaving a ship.

Gantry crane—a movable structure on a dock, with a boom that supports the machinery used for lifting, lowering and moving cargo. A LASH ship has a gantry crane built into its stern.

Hatch—an opening in the deck of a ship. Cargo is loaded through the hatch into the hold.

Hawsepipe—a hole or pipe in the bow of a ship through which a hawser (cable) or anchor chain passes.

Helmsman—the ablebodied seaman who is assigned to steer the ship. On a freighter the helmsman is often referred to as the quartermaster.

Hold—a compartment belowdecks where cargo is stored.

Hull—the shell or frame of a ship.

Liner—a cargo ship that runs on a regular schedule to selected ports.

Longshoreman—a dock worker who loads and unloads ships.

Loran—stands for *Long Range Aid to Navigation*. An electronic instrument that uses radio and radar signals to help navigate a ship.

Merchant marine—a nation's fleet of cargo ships, and the people who work them.

Port—the left side of a ship, facing forward.

Quartermaster—(see **Helmsman**)

Rigging—the masts, booms, ropes and cables that rise above a ship's deck.

Rudder—a flat piece of metal or wood projecting from the stern of a ship. The rudder is used to steer the ship through the water.

Screw—a device with blades that turn in the water and propel a ship forward or backward.

Starboard—the right side of a ship, facing forward.

Superstructure—the structure above the top deck of a ship that houses the bridge, the officers' and crew's quarters, the galley, the ship's stores and machine shops.

Tramp—a cargo ship that runs on an irregular schedule. It is available to pick up and discharge cargo anywhere in the world.

Watch—a four-hour period during which part of a ship's crew is on duty.

Winch—a machine with a horizontal drum around which rope or cable is coiled. A winch is used to raise and lower cargo and equipment.

ACKNOWLEDGMENTS My thanks to the people who so patiently answered my questions, advised me and cooperated in the making of this book: Peter P. Gerquest—Seaquest Chartering, Inc.; Jerry Alfano—Hellenic Lines; Jim Rolfe—Salwico, Inc.; Joseph Strempek—United States Lines; David Gilmartin—United States Lines; James E. Butcher—Hoegh-Ugland Auto Lines; Bill Germinario—Atlantic Container Lines; Laurie A. McFarlin—American Steamship Co.; Sergio G. Rocha Lena, Jorge G. Peredo—Heliservicio Campeche; Lois Johnstone, Darryl Shields, E.H. Whiting III—Texaco; Martha Rowe—Panhandle Eastern Corporation; Captain R. W. Mackintyre and the officers and crew of the ship *Texaco Rhode Island*.